Best wishes,
Betty McKellar

Muirshiel

Betty McKellar

illustrations and maps by Netta Cameron

Muirshiel

Betty McKellar

illustrations and maps by Netta Cameron

Grimalkin Press
2008

Grimalkin Press
19 Currie Place, Cooper's Wynd
Glasgow G20 9EQ

ISBN: 978-09553786-2-1

The publisher acknowledges the financial
assistance of the Lochwinnoch Millennium Events Group and
the Clyde Muirshiel Regional Park.

Copyright: All poems and stories are the copyright of the
respective individual authors in accordance with Section 77 and
78 of the Copyright, Design and Patents Act 1988.

All rights are strictly reserved.
Requests to reproduce the text in whole or in part should be
addressed to the publisher.

All illustrations and maps by Netta Cameron.

Typeset and designed by Grimalkin Press.

Printed by: printing.com@tangerine
49 Cowane Street, Stirling FK8 1JW
Email: stirling@printing.com / Web: www.printing.com

Muirshiel Centre

The Road to Muirshiel

Come Walk with Me

I am very fortunate in this life.
I take the road to Muirshiel every day.
I live at the very heart of our Regional Park, and in this book of poetry I sing the praises of an area of the country that has become mine. But, of course, it's your country too, and in my way I'm urging you to join me in my intense pleasure at belonging to this good earth, along with the birds that fly above us and the creatures of the hills and hedgerows and waterways that live out their lives as we do in a beautiful world.

For me, the road to Muirshiel starts in Lochwinnoch, at our special village landmark, 'Auld Simon'. The plough weather vane of his clock tower rises above the holly and laburnum and yew that choose to grow in ancient graveyards such as his. Artists love him, and he hangs on a hundred village walls.

From Auld Simon onwards it's uphill all the way, but the slopes are gentle and the road so full of interest that you will not tire. Stop at the top of Johnshill and go down the crushed glass track to the lookout point over Castle Semple Loch. A heron from the Hillside heronry might well be making its lazy flightpath to the water, and rooks from the rookery are always active. Good bird-watching here, and it's still just the edge of the village.

Don't be tempted to linger too long at this lovely spot, however, for there are many pleasures ahead. Enjoy the birch trees and the well planned woodland layout at Cruiks. Contemplate the alterations to Jean Sinclair's wee auld hoose at Boghead Toll. At this point, be careful not to veer off towards Kilmacolm. Keep straight on past the cottage and follow the signs for the park. Have an open eye for yellowhammers as you pass the hawthorns at Balgreen. Admire the chestnut horses at Meikle Cloak.

As you turn the corner beyond the avenue of beech trees, you're approaching the open ground of Tandlemuir – the Bonfire Moor. I like to think that once upon a time ancient painted men came up from their lochside crannogs to build the Beltane fires here, and dance their dances round them, in days before history was written down.

It's sheep country today, and you'll probably see the farmer on his quad bike, rounding up Scottish blackfaces or texels in the fields. Farmers don't wear legs nowadays, and even their collie dogs prefer to travel to work on the back spar of a bike. The days of herd laddie boots and the heather loup are long gone.

It's up the brae now, towards Clovenstone. Every year, when I lived here, I'd stand in the garden to listen for curlews in spring and skylarks in summer; fieldfares in autumn and woodpeckers on the bird-table in winter too. They never failed me. This must be one of the most picturesque cottages in Renfrewshire, and 1808 is chiselled into its clubskews. Two hundred years in open moorland, buffeted by all the storms, and still it stands, a fine old Scottish peasant homestead for all of us to admire as we continue on our way towards the Centre.

Look for primroses on the primrose bank above the quarry. Don't go pinching them for your flowerbeds, though; the Rangers don't like it. Instead, raise you eyes upwards to the ruins of Edge. Kestrels and buzzards fly here.

At the Jessie Burn, turn to look back at the view. Smell the flowers; scented thyme and ladies' bedstraw, wild pansies and queen of the meadow. In summer time it's better than Chanel Number 5.

You're nearly there by the time you turn the corner and see Heathfield, a sad rickle of stones now, but ideal shelter for the stoat who likes solitude and lives in the dry stane dyke. If he's not about – little long-nosed shrews.

From Heathfield it's level walking to the Centre. Be careful on the cattle grid between the white gateposts as you enter Muirshiel ground. Enjoy the meadow and the tree plantings and the view of Misty Law. Go to the Centre, talk to the Rangers. Ask about the harriers and the juniper and the history trail.

The homeward trek?

Downhill and easy.

Next time, come by car and make for the heights.

The spirit of Muirshiel will enter your soul.

Betty McKellar.

Beauty Treatment

Auld Simon's had a face-lift.
They've spruced him up
done a spot
of deep-cleansing –
pin-tucks botox detox
he's had the lot.
They just didn't allow that lived-in old face
to crumble away
so he's looking presentable today.

But like a gardener
used to the earth-coloured comfort
of shabbiness
he's not at his ease
not really pleased at being fussed
and brushed
not quite at home in pale grey.

So give him a year
of the weatherings
the bakings and shakings and batterings
from the sun and the wind and the rain.
He'll have reverted
to gravestone hue
grown back
amongst ivy and holly and yew
got patches of moss for his whiskers
he'll not look so new.
In fact
in the main
he'll be just like his old self again.

Auld Simon

Come Sit with Me

Come sit with me
inside this circle on the Hillside height;
breathe in the magic.

Open up the window of your eye
to see
the greyness of the Semple Loch
stretched like a length of satin cloth
below a Lochwinnoch sky
and the grazing sheep and the fat black cows
and the heron bird from the heronry
and many a tall green sycamore tree
in the fields of Renfrewshire.

Now walk the circle, treading light
listening
to whisperings.
Put magic to the circle
like when a faerie woman waves a wand all round herself
and casts a spell.

And draw the voile curtain from your inner eye
for then you can fly
in an old countree
and peer behind shadows to long-ago meadows
and find
an ancient kind
who walked where you walk
and lived and loved
and looked upon a Semple Loch
nearer to when the world began –

hunters of the duck and swan
and Semple Lords
and monks who prayed
and singing boys from the Collegiate Church who sang
a laverock song of praise
for the goodness of the earth;
and Frenchmen from Napoleon's War who carried stone
and built the dyke
that stands below us still, under the hill
staunch as a graveyard statue to their time;
and horsemen riding, trains puffing, cyclists cycling
on a railway-line of spirits
drawn round us on the magic, moving ring of on-going centuries
under Lochwinnoch's sky,
while constant nearby . . .

the greyness of the Semple Loch
stretched like a length of satin cloth
and the grazing sheep and the fat black cows
and the heron bird and the sycamore tree
in the fields of Renfrewshire.

Viewpoint to Castle Semple Loch below Hillside

Birks

The birks that grow
at the Cruiks field-edge
wear skirts o green
that screen their siller skeletons
frae oor een
in the hot sun's rays.
In a' the gowden yallow simmer days
they shimmer and quiver and preen
in thae silken skirts o green.
But when the cauld comes whistlin roon
they drap their green silk claes
an lay them on the groon
an sway their winter dances
wi grey-bone twiglet branches
dreepin doon
like spinly airms
ower winter-white bare nakedness.

Cruicks Farm

Rid Lums at Boghead Toll

Jean Sinclair was a wee Scots wife
an she lived oot a guid Scots life
in her crookit wee hoose
wi its wa's paintit white
an its wee rid lums
an its wee rid door
an its totty rid windaes
ahint an afore.

Noo her dinkie wee hoose
has had a make-o'er
an it's modernised frae the auld days o yore
an prinked til it's braw
frae the roof tae the flair;
but the drawback tae that –
Jean's no there ony mair.

I hope that her ghaist
drifts aboot the new lum
an I hope she approves
o the betterments dune,
for I miss a' the crack
wi the guid auld Scots wife
an the tales o the past
in her guid auld Scots life –
an I miss the rid lums.

Boghead Toll

Due North from Herts.

Plump bosom to the fore
a partridge
proud matron in her summer Sunday clothes
pulled a string of darting pom-poms
over the grass
of a garden in Herts,
nine chicks in all
in babiness
adorable.

Fat mother partridges once could be seen
holidaying
in the long-ago yellow
of corn at the Cloaks
and in cow-parsleyed mellow
of hedgerows and verges and May-fields
by the sweet-smelling hayfields
of Balgreen.

No more.

You babes in the grass
we're due north from Herts.
Take yourselves to the wing, come a-travelling
fly yourselves fast
back up to the past.

Summer with us like before.

Balgreen

Buzzard

The buzzard flies Muirshiel in remote splendour
majestic
wheeling the heights of air
far above the rabble of the lesser kinds
barely aware of nervous chitterings
from abject things
like dunnocks and chaffinches
and starlings
fluttering about the hedges
and the edges of the fields in panic
trying to hide.
He knows they're there
only he won't demean himself
by looking down
from his supreme superiority.
He has better things to do;
he has his own vast world of blue ozone and light
to range and rule.

Every day a little spitfire aeroplane
is sent up high to fight him –
the kestrel in an impetus of hate –
but he's the indestructible airship
that sails an impervious flightpath
regardless of the irritating jabbing
except when he turns over on a slip of weightlessness
to show his talons.

Buzzards and kestrels at the Cloaks

Snowdrops

A glacier of flowers is drifting
down the drive
at the Conveth.
I collaborated with the earth
to get it going
knowing that it might become a whiteness
a delicate stream of lightness
among the bare trees
of March.

From a paltry planting at the hill's crown
the springlet of snow spilled over
feeling its way down
imperceptibly moving
frothing and creeping
reaching out pale-petalled fingers
over the brown-ness of the ground
sliding around the wine-satin bark
of the wild cherry-gean
slipping its tendrils between the beech and the rowan
and the larch.

Twenty years
since I knelt and felt the warmth inside the earth
and listened to the pulsing of the heart of it
touched the blooming on the skin of it
injected life-seed into the core of it –
set in motion my river of flower-snow.

It's growing
and growing
flowing past my time.

Lands of Conveth

The New World

They came to my door
unsure
strangers from Cornwall
looking for roots
in the Tandlemuir.

I knew them.
They've lived in the Tandlemuir lore
over sixty years
grown into the ground with the rest of the stories
like in a tangle of brambles.
They're just one of the branches
fixed to earth core.

They'd left nothing behind
but the legend.

The dairy cattle
their tables and chairs and Sunday dresses
their dogs and cats
their hens
their double beds and mattresses
their children
and their pots and pans and pails –
they'd packed them into carriages
and gone by rail
from Lochwinnoch Station, special train,
"First stop, Cornwall,
all aboard!"
brave as the pioneers of old
in covered wagons
on the road to Oregon
all bound for a New World –
part of the ongoing flow.

The children of their blood
were come
to find them,
respect for what has gone before
in the simple act –
remembrance.

East Tandlemuir

Enough

The first of May:
a clear night with the hint of frost
quite cold
but with the sky horizon-blushed
in pink and pleasurable thoughts
of summer's breath.
My first year here
has come and passed and nearly gone.
I feel the urge
to light a fire
of debris
in my cottage-garden wilderness.

Soon, dry twigs crackle
sparks spit out
flames flicker and leap high.
I throw and poke and prod until its heart glows white
and stand back as heat sears me
strangely satisfied.

Tandlemuir –
the Bonfire Moor.

Pagan men who danced round Beltane flame
and named this place
came
and vanished on a summer's breath.
"Light the fire,
dance the dance,
taste the goodness of the earth."

It is enough.

The Cottage, Mid-Tandlemuir

Bats

Summer twilight;
garden perfumed
as a boudoir heavy-scented with the sweet oils of amour
sky crepesculed
and the moon's face fallen to lop-sided Mona Lisa smile
suffusing the cream discs of the elder flower
to pale splotches of a misty white.

I am beguiled
to well-being
deep-breathing in the benisons of the night.

Then a flicker of black
darts like the touch of a hurt on the face of the moon
and is gone
but in my head
the quivering of bats' wings
and whisperings . . .

Tandlemuir House

Alison's Rescue Service

Every year
it dries up in the ditch
like a beached jelly fish,
protoplasm
black-cell-flicked.

She scoops it up
and tips it in a pail,
drenches it with water from the pond
infused with green,
puts stones between.

A hundred minuscule batteries respond
fuel-fed
kick-started,
ticking
thriving
metamorphosing
diving
cannibalising
under-water jiving.

And then
miraculously
tadpoles are frogs
tiny as though they'd been designed
in Lilliput.

She takes them in her pail
to the safe frog pool
and sets them free
in the deep brown cool.

West Tandlemuir

Herds

Talk about breeds o countrymen
an gey sune
ye'll come up wi
"Herds".

Lang syne they walkit ower the lang miles o the steep hill face
wi collie dugs close in ahint the feet o them
their boots an crook an heather loup
a' pairt o them.
They belangt tae the moorland
like the whaup that nests there in the simmer
or the nervous grouse that fills the August sky
wi its warnin cry
"Gaeback gaeback gaeback . . ."
Herds turnt yowes up on their feet when they got coupit
an saw that silly lambs got sookit.
They dosed them for their ills and jagged their veins
an gaithered stock yowes to get tuppit
wi guid strains
o sturdy rams.
They kennt ilk beast like ye wad ken yer freends
an at the back end in the Lanark sales
they balanced oot the points o them
an argie-bargied wi their kind what was the best o them
an shook their heids aye at the price o them.
No muckle's chainged,
only they've rummelt up the pace on that hill face.
Noo they're fast.
They zoom and bump a path on wheels high on the braes.
These days they like
to ride
a Kawasaki bike.

Farming at West Tandlemuir

Game Bird

For one long glorious summer
a pheasant flew to us from out the skies
and tried
to be a robin.

We called him 'Cocky'.
He came all dignity and swagger in his superiority of size
with his silly-lilly-frilly eyes
and his trails of tails
and his feathers glowing bronze and fawn and gold
instead of red
and his little bird-brain well-concealed
inside a little irridescent green-jewel head.

He made us laugh.
He was an air-bus to a spitfire in manoeuvrability
an aero-dynamic improbability.
He'd have needed helicopter-blades fixed to his head
to land on our bird-table
and claim his robin prize.
He was only able for the dyke nearby.
He always looked ridiculously surprised
when he stretched out his scrawny neck too far
and lost his balance like a fat gymnast on the bar
toppling towards the ground
in a squawking embarrassment of outraged pheasant sound
crash landing
smoothing himself down
settling for fallen robin pickings that he found.

And then one day our pheasant friend had gone,
the bird had flown
he'd had enough, was in a huff.
He'd given up
on trying to be
a robin.

We'd enjoyed him for a summer
but we forgot him
until Shirley and Billy and Jeff and Willie Webb
came from the Tandlemuir Shoot
triumphantly hot-foot.
"Look what we've got,
one for the pot,
a present for you,"
was what they said.
This time we enjoyed him
gastronomically.

And should you shudder and condemn the likes of me,
and point the finger
accusatorially –
think of that chicken you're eating for your tea.

Then think of Cocky
who was for a summer gloriously free
trying to be
a robin.

Shooting on Tandlemuir ground

Summer 2003

God smiled
pulled back the curtain of the clouds
for His summer show,
switched on the lighting . . .
and we had a sighting of Him
a full glow
of miracle.
The cheeks of girls bloomed apricots from the brightness
little old ladies absorbed ease into their cores from warmness
so that their brittle bones remembered the 1940s
and tangoed them
onto the kitchen floor.

Sunshine and heat.
He floated them into the breeze
touched the air to turquoise
covered bare branches in green cloaks
set choirs of lark sopranos singing
and laughing cuckoo echoes ringing
from the oaks.
He threw down butterflies in showers
of colour
painted flowers
deeper than ever before
pink to red
yellow to gold
blue to indigo.
"All's right with the world,"
He told us.

On another stage a bomb explodes. *Clovenstone*

"Think," He whispers in our ears,
"Look and see.
Now, choose how your world
is going to be . . ."

Jean and Gail and the Tawny Owl

In the secret-passage hollow
of an ash
beyond the Clovenstone
a tawny owl is nesting.
Today its cache was rumbled
by the children
tree-climbing.
The bird came tumbling out at them
in fright
wakened from its daytime sleep
to startled flight.

Later
when the girls had recovered breath
and the sun had sunk below the west horizon
and a slim new crescent moon
had risen
sharp as a sickle in the sky
and mankind had retreated to orderly square nest-boxes
in town,
a dark bird-shadow flew above the cottage chimneys
on a haunting
flaunting its dented bravado
smoothing its ruffled feathers down.

Tu wit tu woo
tu wit tu woo
tu wit tu woooo, it said
so human and persistent
that for an instant unease flickered in us
and we locked up and got ready for our bed.

The ash tree above Clovenstone

Plight of Ravens

Would they desecrate the stronghold of the ravens?
Would they defile the wild grey crags
of Turnave Hill
where great bird hobos
cast their colours
in a raggedness of black
and dance their gaberlunzie ballet
like whirlwind acrobats
on blasts of air
that take them on dust-devil highs
to unfurl their raven wings like banners
on the wide blue Muirshiel skies?

A raven fortress
stone
that stands its guard
above the Muirshiel moss and heather:
is this where they would plant
their gaunt white tree
whose trunk is bare bone
and arms brute hard?
Its hand
will fell the gaberlunzie bird
and the raven heart will drip black blood
on moorland floor.
There will be moaning on the wind
where ravens soar.

What are they,
who would desecrate the stronghold of the ravens?

Turnave Hill is threatened with wind turbines

Listen for the Skylarks

It's springtime
so I walked along the moorland road
at Edge
to listen for the skylark song.

It was there
hanging on the air like sun shimmering on sea,
fizzy sherbet bursts of sound.
But grandchildren had come with me
a brass band
making its own music.

"Shush! listen for the skylark song," I hissed
but they laughed on, unaware.

The old gate hung on hinges
locked in rust like my arthritic hip.
We had to climb.

The children leapt like deer
arms to the sun in the clear air.
Movement in itself was joy.

I eased myself across
painfully.
Youth has it all, I thought . . .

but then
    I've got
        the skylarks.

Edge

Primroses

The primroses are out,
tucked under damp boulders
by the Calder Burn.

Where they're hidden
in the steep parts of the Glen
in nooks and crannies among ash and hazel
we see them come in careless abandonment,
flower waterfalls of yellow
like cream spilling from a jug overturned.

But the roadside at the well-known bank
where once they flourished
is quite bare.
They're dotted bleakly there in sparse clusters
reluctantly pretty
holding in their charms
against raiding gardeners
with their trowels at the ready
to plunder them.

Primrose Bank

The Troot

I guddled a troot frae the Jessie Burn,
I sat on my hunkers an kittled its tum,
I reached doon my airm in the dark dark pool
ablow muckle stanes in the deep deep cool.

It wriggelt an wiggelt an tried tae get free
then it shoogelt an gey near escapit frae me,
but I jinkit it high tae glint in the sky
an it tummelt its wulkies –
I laughed wi the fun;
it cam doon on the grund by the Jessie Burn.

O my wee brither was jealous o me
cos there wasnae anither troot for tae see!

The Jessie Burn

The Sly Way In

When they stripped the country's elm trees
to the bone
so that they shivered on the horizon
like shamed Jews
naked from the Holocaust,
they missed the one at Heathfield.
It stayed dressed
in leafiness
summer after summer.

Full blooming beautiful it was
in its well-being.
You could smell the breath of health from it
like from a rain-touched garden,
lift its sweeping branches from the earth
and creep
under the voile parasol
to an enclosed wholesomeness of green,
a theatre of sweet airs
where blackbirds sang their hearts out from the gods.

But last year's leaves were crinkle-edged
and spotted brown like pensioners' old hands.
The bark is peeling.

Death
is feeling its sly way in.

Heathfield

Morning Walk

Today I walked to Brownie's Linn.
It was the morning time
the time of freshness in the spring smell of the wind
the time of April birds
singing their early lovesongs in the budding rowans.
I looked down from the carpark through the trees
and saw the rippling ribbon of the Calder
going its way,
felt drawn to it
went down the rustic steps,
scrunched through shells from yesterday
that spoke of children
rolling eggs in Easter play,
went down the slope
past shelters for their barbecues
through the gate to reach the path
that took me beside the river with its water running fast.
I walked with the flow
enjoying the bluster of the teasing air
blowing through the wildness of my resentful hair
to the Waterfall,
saw the wildness of the river as it leapt
the boiling and the frothing and the writhing
the water-mist rising,
watched it settle and rest, and slide on smoothly to the river depths
making for Semple Loch.

Just a walk
but it set my blood like river water flowing
got me going
for the day.

The Brownie's Linn on the River Calder

Whisperer to the Breeze

They tell me there's a green man hiding
in the cover of the Muirshiel trees.
Someone saw him
gliding round the shafts of them
sliding behind the trunks of them
a mysterious ghost-man
a whisperer to the breeze.

As he goes floating in the sunshine of their glades
and flitting through the dimness of their shady places
he stops to stroke the bark of them
murmur into the dark of them
touch fingernails of green on the long slim arms and hands of them
and in the heart of them
there comes a surging of earth juices
and they breathe

and then the spring and summer move in billowing waves of lushness
high above him
and flowers smile up and quiver for they love him
and the grasses and the mosses
and the rushes shiver pleasure and desire.
"Sing!" he shouts to the blackbirds
"Sing!" to the robins and the thrushes
and birds and trees and flowers and grasses sing together
in the Green Man's choir.

Muirshiel Centre

Spirit of Muirshiel

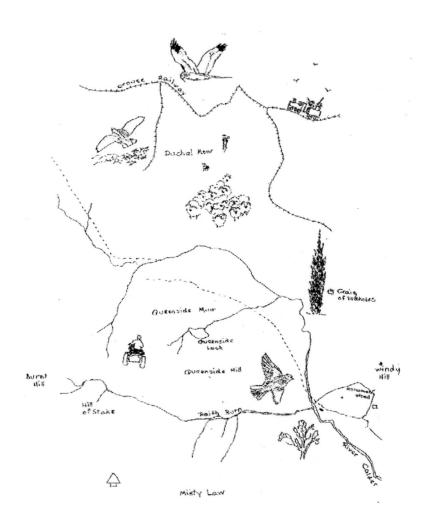

Rites of Spring

Look high above the grand arena
of our Muirshiel moorland.
The white Nijinsky dancer
is taken to the blue
in a solo matinee –
incandescent star
gliding and leaping
to the wild Stravinsky music of the planet's breathing
soaring on the impetus
of his life-force choreography.

Let your spirit surge and rise and whirl;
dance with the fierce white dancer,
join in his glee.
The age-old singing of the heart
starts up
in all the radiant earth's glad lonely places
and shouts
"Be free!"

Yallow

Yallow's a licht that braks through a smirrin o grey,
it's a sun ray
dancin wi' green.

It's primroses spilt ower the heid o a bank
in a tummlin glut
clottit
like poored oot cream.

Yallow's the fuzz on the back o a bumbee
bumlin in flooer rosettes,
it's a yorlin burd up amang poothery hazel catkins
singin its best.

It's daffodil ladies blawin their trumpets unner a tree.
It's a kiss frae the air
a smirkle in Averile's ee.

The Path that Came Down from the Sky

Larks make filigree music in a silver laverock choir
and the clarsach wind seuchs rhythms
to soft airs from Windy Hill
whispering enchantments
in a day of Maytime highs
as we walk the magic pathway that came down from out the skies.

And white bog cotton wisps
and sways in faerie puffs of cotton fluffs
and dotted on the moorland grass
like minuscule bulbs of rich stained glass
are luscious crimson blaeberry flowers
fallen in crimson raindrop showers.
The air is perfume, vaporised,
and away towards Queenside a harrier flies
as we walk the magic pathway that came down from out the skies.

And down from the summit of Windy Hill heights
the far-away world is a glory of lights
with its shimmering windows and roofs and spires
and the hills all around are on sun-gold fire
as the larks and the wind reach crescendo
and we feel in our hearts that we're harmonized
the goodness of Earth a reward and a prize . . .

so walk the magic pathway that came down from out the skies.

The walk to Windy Hill

Words in Green Silk

Her needle sewed a picture from my words.
My words gleamed silk
and they were coloured in a greenwood green
satin-silvered in a sheen
of delicate embroidery.
I looked
and marvelled,
listening to familiar whisperings in my head
and heard
the soundless rustlings of a wakening spring
in threads
of dew
rising through the veins of Muirshiel trees
in trickling filaments of liquid willow green.
And from between the wisps of verdant leaves
there gazed
that ancient green-man face
that comes from where the world began
and summons out
the heart-beat surge
of April birds
and flowers and grass and age-old oak and ash
and beats its rhythm in the deep earth-soul of man.

Words and silken thread
poet-artist meld
a mutual giving.

for Christine Mackenzie

The Purple Time

August is the purple time
the lush time
the luscious time
with the road-edge tangled in a mass
of summer's last wild rampant rasps
over-ripe with sweet, bruised fruit
that trickles down its mulled-wine juice
for thirsty, intoxicated thrushes.
And there's the fankle of the bramble bushes
with berries
darkening to a shine
for next month's bramble-berry time.

And struggling out from this melee
triumphantly
come knapweed
and mauve scabious
and fat pink clover flowers all blushing
and from a patch
of just the grass
a scattered shower of purple pansies
held over from the July high-noon blooming.

Autumn's coming.
But while there's time still
look to the Queenside hill.
She's covered in hot heather flushes
of purple
for in the year's circle
August
is the purple time.

The Scarlet an the Green

Liquid siller drifts low doon frae the coracle o a Michaelmas mune
that traivels the lift on a gossamer sail
an lichts the warld
frae a storm-lamp trail.
Inside she cairries the Autumn Queen
wha sprinkles her magic shimmer sheen
abune the scarlet an the green.

Touch the scarlet
touch the green
wi yer lang white fingur o faerie gleam,
reach frae yer boat tae the faur ablow
an gloss the harvest in ripeness glow
wi a lilly-lowe an a lilly-lowe
on rodden scarlet
an aipple green
an the bourtree bush that bides atween.

rodden - rowan
aipple - apple
bourtree - elder

For magic wine frae the Autumn Queen
simmers on in the scarlet an the green
so gaither them in
tae yer basket's brim
tak as mony as ye can win,
add sugar crystal tae their core,
the Autumn Queen has a fruitfu store,
an when winter seuchs in wi his cauld grey wheeze
an grips ye in his icy squeeze
ye'll melt tae the sweetness o what has been
in the fruits that were touched by the Autumn Queen
the rodden scarlet
an aipple green
an the bourtree bush that bides atween.

Centre Pin

When I was young
and the sun shone in my sky
I climbed on the Hill of Stake
and the Misty Law.
I remember that I saw the Paps of Jura
lolling in the seas beside Kintyre.
Further down was Ayr
and a secret faerie island –
Ailsa Craig
my Bali Hai –
then Galloway and Kirkcudbrightshire.
Lanark was there
turned to blueness in the faraway air
and I was seeing
block graphs of buildings
and triangular spires
in a conglomerate of towns
by Paisley.

This was being.
I was an eagle flier
soaring
on the top of Renfrewshire.
Centre pin
in the round of earth and sea?
ME!

I'm back to base.
I took a tumble down the hill face of the years
and the wise eagle
knows its place.

A Muirshiel Cloning

Once upon a time
they used the wood of juniper
to light their fires
breathing in
its aromatic fragrance
and knowing they were safe
in the little huts of stone
because its freshness warded off the spirits.
Wise old women learnt to use its berries
in their brews
and then the entrepreneurs
invented gin.
Juniper was 'in'.

But times change.
Our fires no longer burn.
Now we flick a switch and heat comes on.
On the hills the juniper has declined;
gin-makers are searching for berries
to flavour that juniper wine.
So . . .

They came to Muirshiel
where one hardy juniper
holds on against the whistling wind
clinging by its roots
solitary as the monk in the wilderness
a recluse
gritting its teeth
and surviving.

They want it to stay
in its wilderness way
and multiply.
They want a hundred Muirshiel junipers
under the Muirshiel sky.

Scientists are nipping it
fingertipping it
horticulturally cloning it
planting it
caring for it like it was Dolly,
watching its growth.
There's hope.
They promise a blooming on the moor
from this one juniper source,
and then . . .

a gush of distillation
enough to satisfy the nation,
so all those who favour a G and T
be thankful for Muirshiel's juniper tree.

Scottish Blackfaced Sheep

A poem about a sheep?
"Don't try to write one," the writers said.
"Sheep are not the stuff
of poetry."

And yet . . .
when rams are gathered close
in a field corner
with curved horns
carved around their faces
and their heads held high –
there's something of the Viking
in their eye.

And when the yowes whirl fast
to mother their lambs
and stamp their feet
and face up to the predatory fox
that slinks in sly
behind them
for a snatch
at weaklings,
they're a match
for the Viking rams.

And when their lambs
gather together at the hillock's crest
on April evenings
when the sun is a rosy blush
towards the west –
that's the best,
for then there's the mad joy-rush
of play and run.
They're rollicking snow-boarders
flying down the green
in child-like fun.

I think, then, maybe
that Scottish blackfaced sheep
can figure
in poetry.

Gentry

Collie dogs have taken
to mechanisation.
They travel by Honda bike
on the back spar
with noses up
like gentry in a car,
chauffeur-driven.

Ilk Year

anither spring will come . . .
laverocks will trill their music to the hert-beat o the lift
the mavis and the blackie on the ash will join in the lilt
whaups gargle descants.

Yowes swalt heavy will be walkit, cannily
doon frae the high hill
for the udderlocking.
They'll graze the herby parks ablow the heather line
an drap their lambs in the rough grass
an lick the steam frae the bluid-smeart wool o them
an gie them sook.
Collie dugs will slink
sleekit-like
amang the glut o cleanins
an jouk the herd's buit.

Heartsease

Come June
they break free of the coarse grass under Windy Hill,
tiny hearts
quickened and pleasured and purple-flushed
by the touch of a sunray,
evanescent as love's first blush.

They come like in the scatter from a summer bride,
floretted confetti
amongst the pearly bedstraw and the golden tormentil,
each one a digit
infinitesimal
in the sum total beneficence
of the June bouquet.

Daur

It's an "afore it's ower late" recklessness
frae the brave new hip
a loupin in tae ilka day
thankrife
a wakenin frae the deid.

It's the clim
doon that crag face
aside a linn o watter
frothy as the veil o a bride
wind-skiffed,
soople rodden brainches for the rope
tae dreep ye –
a hingin spider on its threid –
in tae a world o emerald moss
an star-white dots o sourock
ablow trees
whaur even the air ye breathe is faerie green
an the river narrows rin
as rich an broon
as yer life-bluid, through Earth's vein . . .

The cave is in there
secretfu' as yer ain soul
gey near beyond the reach
whaur a smeddum ye didna ken was yours
is bidin, deep.

The Cave by the Calder

Harrier

It was a fly-past
a display.
The air ace of the moor
appeared
on cue,
no camouflage
he flew
majestically,
a pride of white
against the rock and sky
a swoop of light
towards the heathland grey
the harrier flight.

"Gobackgobackgoback" –
frights of sound
resonate,
panics echo in staccato
from the scuttering grouse.

But he will stay.
In this wide Muirshiel world
he is the Lord
of all that he surveys.

And in her hidden place
his mate
settles
on the future,
all yellow-glitter watchfulness
aware
of eyes
lasering
the air.

Sangsters

Laverocks play the clarsachs o the air
they're speerits o music
ris up chord on chord for ilka note they sing
pu'in on crescendo strings o their ain herts
until they're brak wi sweetness
in the gowden reaches
o the heaven's airts.

Selkies seugh the hert-beat o the sea
greetin their saft grey tear-draps wi the waves
ripplin intil melody
an crashin
mournfu sounds like cymbals
agin the derk clift wa's
o hollow caves.

Gledness – dool.
Twa pairts heich an laich o the choir sang.
In atween
we pitch oorsels
agin the plains o earth
whaur we maun gang.

This poem was the inspiration for Sally Beamish's concerto 'Sangsters'.

History of Muirshiel

Muirshiel House

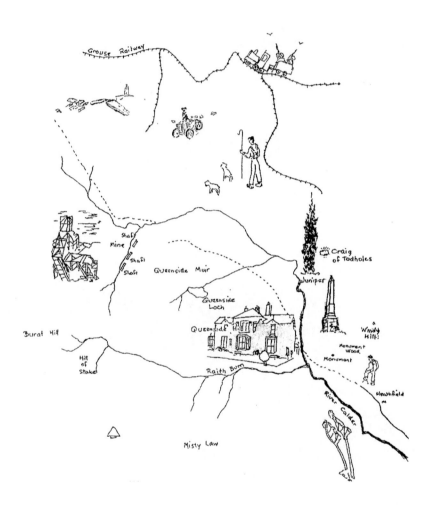

The Chiffon Time

Come walk with me into the chiffon time
of my remembrancing
to see the ones who once have been
grey mist dancers from the far-away
behind the filmy screen
shimmerings
that sigh on a wind-breath of the in-between
behind a translucent magic
of quivering Muirshiel green.

One day we'll fade with all those shadow dancers
to the misty grey of the far-away.
Tremors of air
we'll be
the ones who once have been
pulled over
beyond the magic Muirshiel green
to move to old tunes in all the ancient rhythms
prisms
glimmering in the joined-hand line
that passes through time.

Carved in Stone

There's a man who lies asleep
among the rhododendron trees
in the wood
on the hill
above Muirshiel.
If by chance you find him
whisper as you pass
and walk on gently
so that you do not shake and shiver him in his bones.
He lies in his chosen quiet place
held in the rooted arms of an ancient tree
his life carved out in stone.

In his time he was the steward of Muirshiel –
not 'owner'
for no one man can really own such ground –
and now an enchanted Muirshiel forest grows around him
like a faerie spell
so you will find it hard to reach him.
Better to walk on by
and feel his spirit vibes
that drift forever with the soaring birds
that range the Muirshiel sky.

Some of the carved letters are already crumbled
on his obelisk stone,
an ongoing decay.
There will come a day
when all the writing on the stone is rubbed away
to dust
by time's storms,
then even the name of him will be gone –
nothing to say
that Lord Francis Nathaniel Conyngham
walked this earth
and served his time
from birth to death.

Fighting Back

Nearly forty years since the McKellars
moved from Heathfield
and the bulldozers breenged in
to lay it low.

There's been no healing to its wound.
The gaps are raw and sore,
jagged, open
crying outrage still,
the stone walls not yet ready to collapse
and 'coorie doon'
into the role of scenic ruin.

What was a neat patch
of parsley, golden wonders,
geometric cabbage rows
is now a sea of nettle
flowing strong into the shore of moorland grass
with the corrugated iron flotsam of a nissen hut
which housed the tups
one more reminder of a living past.

Beyond the dyke
even the birds have flown.
Where once there was the peewit cry
the drum of snipe, the blackcock dance,
there's empty sky.
Only the sad wind
whistles and sighs and moans.

But one thing soldiers on
the rhubarb.
Rhubarb fights back.
It wins the annual battle against nettle,
grows tall and strong and rampant red and fat.

Every year I gather it.
Every year McKellars lick their lips
in pink juice from my rhubarb tarts.
Old Archie McKellar's ghost still barks
"Heathfield rhubarb?
The best rhubarb in Renfrewshire!"

The Sheep Fanks

The fanks below the Windy Hill are silent now.
They died.
No clippings here,
no dippings,
rarely a sheep inside . . .

But once upon a sun-drenched July noon
I carried a baker's basket
with egg rolls for the herds
and scones and jam
over the fields from Heathfield
to these fanks.
The air reverberated bleatings,
sheds were a heaving mass of sheep pressed close, steaming,
reeking sheep smells.

I remember it well
the clipping time
the annual gathering of the neighbours.
They came from miles around to contribute their skills
warming to each others' news and banterings
barely stopping for their breathing
keeping up speed
clipping sheep for sheep
eyes askance to see nobody drew too far ahead
faces red and sweaty
in the activity and heat
the old boys dragging in
the next poor candidate for shaving.

Affronted yowes baaed outrage
at the belly-up indignity of the shear
and then leapt clear
skittishly
sideways on their feet
like stylish ladies divested of their furs.
Everywhere laughter, camaradie, teasing, the routine curse;
and whirlwinds of movement –
children climbing in to strung-up woolbags
to tread fleece,
little ones picking up pooks
collie dogs darting for a surreptitious nip
or jouking the boot . . .

Another age.
In the drone of a machine that other world died.
But once upon a July noon those sheep fanks were alive.

Alec

Collie dogs and sheep were all his company
in the treeless landscape beyond Muirshiel.
He walked the hill-tracks there for thirty years
as much a part of the wide moor
as the March curlew keening her banshee cry
or the nervous grouse in August
scuttering from the Queenside heather
with a "Gobackgobackgoback."

He was an Islay man.
Maybe the blueness of his eyes
came from shepherd generations gone before
who had absorbed turquoise
from the Hebridean air,
but every year
their colour intensified and deepened with our Renfrew sky
on lambing mornings
in April and in May
as his skin grew browner from the weather.
I still can see them
smiling their knowing smile
of content.

"Cum by tae ma fit," he'd shout
and stretch out his crook
for the dogs to answer
as he shepherded the flock towards the fanks
or rescued a yowe who'd coupit
or helped a silly lamb to sook.

He died on the hill.
We found him lying
with the dogs whimpering at his side.
The eyes had closed.
"It's juist how he'd have wanted it to be,"
they said of him.
"Sheep an collie dugs were a' he kent."

But once upon a time he'd been a soldier
blue eyes peering from beneath a busby
changing guard at Buckingham Palace,
and in that other life
he'd seen pale corpses of unwanted girl babies
floating down the Yangtse,
flotsam
like the flower from his funeral wreath
drifting on the Raith.

Semmits

Say the words 'semmits'
an I smell sweit still
      reekin
frae unner men's oxters.
Fermers wore semmits tae feed beasts
an herds tae kep sheep
an drainers
      smeekin
on June days when the sun was het
an dykers
an whiles a vet
at the caulvin
wi his airm up a coo's erse.
Semmits were for men wi hairy chests
an biceps
bulgin frae their labours
faithers
grandfaithers
maist o the Scots
that washed theirsels
at the jawbox
afore mince an tattie denners.

Peelie-wally office boys
wore vests.

A Word o Praise

Twa muckle horse
were keepit on the ferm lang-syne
afore the time o the grey Ferguson –
great, strang craiturs
that moved thegither wi' a slow-motion rhythm
a' grace an harmony.
They were gey wise,
kent fine hoo tae gang gentle-like
atween the chains
an answer tae the rein
while the fermer steadied the ploo.
The furrows they churned ower were stracht lines
like the streetched warp threid
on a fu' length o Border tweed
broon, wi grey pooks o stane.

Paddy an Billy –
a photograph was ta'en o them
so we can glimpse them
as they were,
ae black
ae white
age misted.

But for this
the beasts would hae vanished
in the nicht o oor forgettin.
Naebody ploos oor high, thin groon these days
it's no worth the effort
for a' that their willin herts
ance pu'ed an wrastled an gied their a'
at juist a word o praise,
for the betterment o't.

for Quintin

Muirshiel Mining

They took it from the earth
digging into a blackness underneath the moor
to find the seam –
not gold
nor silver
but a rock
pink as the stone in Petra's rose-red city,
fired in some primeval furnace
by the mighty underworld gods
who welded atoms
into stone and minerals and gems
before our world began.

Treasure enough
for man
to appropriate
in an industrial age –
barytes
they called it
and worked
in a cruel black hole
to find it.

The earth gave
as the earth gives
and men took what the earth gives
as man always takes,
and the lorries plied their east-west way
up and down the road
until one day
they took the last barytes load away
and earth lay back
exhausted.

Now there is a barren-ness
where once men from our village worked the mine,
the sense of a hurt to the landscape.
A few pink stones and pebbles, lying randomly
show what once has been.
Props have collapsed
debris settled in.
Earth
recuperates slowly.
Mostly, an eerie silence.
Somewhere near
you'll sometimes hear young peregrines
crying
from a secret nest.

And man?
He moves on
seeking alternatives.

Hard to Find

If you walk up to the Duchal Moor
from Muirshiel
you'll have to keep looking, hard
to find the old Grouse Railway.
It's out there
way beyond the Todholes
hiding somewhere
beneath the middle of nowhere.
But persevere –
Ordinance Survey has it down;
it can be found.

Mostly, of course,
the bog has swallowed it up
into the glaur of its guts.
But you get glimpses;
a rusted rail
all wrapped in mosses
crosses the burn like a bridge
disappears
in a rampage of heather
juts out again free of the ruts
quite near
to the line of the butts.

Now use your imagination.
Think of the toffs.
Doff your hats as they pass
shoogling their way to the Glorious Twelfth
over the shined-up tracks.
All to have fun with the gun –
they'll not likely return;
today you'll see harriers
you'll not hear "Go backs".

Grouse
are harder to find
than the Railway.

Bound to the Ground

When the keepers move in line behind the birds
and the guns crack sharp staccato down the glen
it seems as if the grasses sway and come to life
and whisper secretly
within the breeze-talk of the air
of seasons long-since gone on the Queenside.

Ghosts are there.
They're bound to the ground forever
like the heather and the grouse and the old shepherds
and the blackfaced sheep
stirred from sleep by our remembering –
all the lairds and gamekeepers generations back
Jack Maclay and Howards and Fletchers
Tommy Fowler, Peter Clark.

Each in his time held fast
to a tradition
that stretches like a touch-rope from the past.
Quintin and Sean and John Phillips will join them.

Muirshiel House 1939

Marigold Mirabelle Miriam Miranda
Martin and Mark and Michael and Miles
come for the shooting
Howards
from London
bright birds of paradise
all swank and style.

Miranda and Miriam Mirabelle Marigold
Miles and Martin and Michael and Mark
up for the season
grouse is the reason
Howards of Glossop
all game for a lark.

Farmers and gamekeepers
dance to their music
housekeeper gardeners
butler and maids
dykers and ditchers
all jerked on their puppet-strings.
Lairds on a visit?
We're all being paid.

Highest society not much sobriety
champagne and dancing
life lived for fun
gaiety laughter
never mind after
Hitler is aiming his gun.

From Beyond the Windy Hill

As though a bride
all sequined
from some strange faerie place beyond the Hill
had thrown a wedding scattering around
the strands of silver tinkled down
drifting, quivering
light as the shiverings of air.
They reached the ground
in purple night shimmerings
and stayed 'til day
and lay in tinsel glimmerings
on heather moors
in spaces in the arms of trees
and by the cottage doors
bright metal glinting against dour gray.

Children dived for slivers of the silver
in this mysterious treasure-scramble from on high.
Their mothers and their fathers lifted up their eyes
      wonderingly . . .
      no planes
      an empty sky.

Vitamin C

Scarlet bright as candle-light inside the red glass lanterns
on old-time Christmas trees
the rose-hips flaunt their brazen beauty
by the roadside edge.
Like brash bead jewellery on Lorelei arms
they sway
seductively,
waving at passing thrushes
from the winter hedge.
"Touch me
taste me
take me," they sing
to the fieldfares and the shy redwing.

Today we leave the rose-hips to the birds
bird bread.
We have our oranges and grapes and peaches
tangerines
pomegranates
Mackintosh reds.
Our children's lips taste sweet with juice
from the world's fruit.

But in the War we picked them crimson-ripe
shiny gems.
We garnered them
in little punnet boxes made of shavings
saving the goodness in them,
lasering their absorbed sun rays
into bottles of liquid health
to infuse pinched baby faces
with pink rose
from the generous earth.

Any we found
penny a pound.

The Land-Girl

6 a.m.
Outside – the dark.
Winter haps her smir of icy mist on the slate roofs.
A swoop of white wing onto the rafters of the cave barn
high above the kennel
and the dog lets out a bark.
But stillness is on the stone face of the farm.

In its heart
dim light from the byre storm lamp
and the stir of morning;
damp cows steaming from the warmth of sleep
risen from their bed
their noses deep in the summer meadow sweetness of hay,
snuffling contentment
horns tossing the neat grass bundles to an easy looseness.

Milking-time.
The clatter of a pail.
Wee May
beamed out from Govan
to an alien land
and with a line in city glamour
in the angle of the snood over her head
is hunkered on the stool below the belly
of an Ayrshire cow.
Her brow rests on its brown flank.
She's served her time.
Able hands, work-red
pull at the fat pink sausage teats
and hot milk froths in the luggie.
She's learnt to keep it steady in between her knees
against past spills from restless animal feet.
But she's tired still, her eyes not clear of sleep.

She's dreaming
her lips still tasting of her last night's kissing.
For her it's yesterday.
Her eyelids droop
the rhythm of her pulling slows
and falls away.

She startles to the farmer's voice.
"Get on with the milking, wee May!"

The Slipe

At the far end of the garden, by the wooden shed
it lay among nettles
neglected
forgotten.
Geraniums in terracotta pots flowered on it
brash red.
"Grandpa," came the shout,
"Look what I've found.
It's a big sledge."

For the old man
memory flashed
clear as glass.
It was the War again.

The slipe.
He saw old Paddy standing there attached to it,
homely farm horse
dressed
like he'd been bred to pull a hearse.
He'd groomed him to be gleaming on that day
had polished up the leather saddlery and brass.
Together they'd pulled it all the way from Heathfield,
through the snow
up the Mine Road to the moor
above the icy Calder Dam.
The beast was willing like his kind.
Wartime made his load a heavy one.
Today for him was just another hard day on the farm.

But it was soldier lads
who'd carried up the corpses from the crash
over the carpet of bleak white.
They'd placed them, gentle-like
and tied them, three cold statues frozen to stone
on the slipe.

He'd led the horse back down the wintry road
slow and easy
with a dignity inbred.
Swingle trees had jingled a sad funeral tune.
The men had walked respectfully behind
eyes to the ground in honour of the dead.

"Grandpa, IS it a sledge?"
"Come and I'll tell you the story," the old man said.

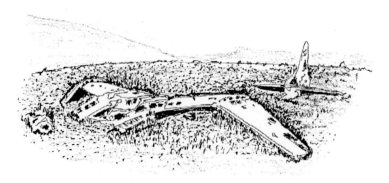

Heat Shimmerings

The edges of Mistylaw trembled and merged into sky.
It was a day of high heat shimmerings
a world heather-flushed in the balm of summer
calm.
A single gull flew lazily towards the dam at Queenside
dallying and gliding
on warm breaths of air
and a shepherd was there surveying his landscape
the ewes and their half-grown lambs all contentedly grazing
or sleeping
August-drowsed
steeped in well-being.

Seeing the woman
driving the pony and governess cart
floating towards him
was like seeing a mirage.
She came from nowhere
a stranger
was suddenly there at the moorland's heart
with her white pony pawing the ground
and her eyes sad-sweet
dark night deep as water in the brown peat pools.
"Where did the plane come down?"
she wanted to know.

And on the moor there was snow
the white-out that shut out his light
on that night in the War years ago.
He remembered the power of the gale
blowing the sleet in his face
cruel
stinging his skin;
and the sound –
he could still hear the sound in his ears
feel the fear like a flapping black bat in his core,
the wounded roar of the plane
flying nearer and nearer towards him
up on the Windyhill ground

O it was low
as low as the trees,
he could almost have touched it
he had cringed to his knees from the fear of it.
Then the din of the crash
like a cannon shot flash in his head.

He had found the wreck gripped in ice,
on the Queenside
inside
a boy
staring . . .
O it was too sad for bearing
a sight to keep in the midnight-black depth of his soul.

As the woman looked down
he gazed into her eyes
and he knew.
They were his eyes . . .

And then it was summer again.
He showed her the patch where only the white heather grew.
He saw that she wept and he left her
alone
a woman bereft.

His ewes and their half-grown lambs grazed on
or slept
August-drowsed
in a world heather-flushed in the balm of summer
peaceful and warm.
Horizons shimmered
sun shone . . .

Heathfield's Old Oak Table

Once in the War
all the evacuees at Heathfield
crept below the old oak table
and huddled in like rabbits scuttled into a burrow
hiding their eyes in fright –
the night the Germans flew above Muirshiel
in monster planes
with engines roaring like angry dinosaurs on wings,
and dropped out bombs on the hill side
short of the target
at the shipyards of the Clyde.
All of the glass windows shattered and shot around
in ice spears,
but nobody was hurt
not a cut nor a scrape of the skin.
The old table did them proud
and stood firm.

Six generations of the family
it's gone through
from the time of Victoria.
Ca' the handle
and it opens itself wide
for spare boards to get put in the inside
and take the family hordes
like a comfortable old granny
holding out her arms for more bairns.
White damask linen over it for the Christmas scene,
sixteen place settings,
McKellar faces beaming over the turkey
and the clootie dumpling
in an illustration from a Dickens novel.
There's been a century of such homely pleasures round this table.
Who can gauge
the value and the strength it's given?

Boundaries

No artist sat down to design them
yet they are pencil-scored across the landscape
like an architect's plans.

They evolved
from peasant knowledge
of the fields, the marshes,
the massive shoulders of the hills
their cliffs and dips and rises,
and from man's need
of boundaries.
Through all the bitter winters
they survive
and function in their roles.
They hold the farms and steadings and the cottages
in stony arms
and on the hill
sheep use them for a bield.

Throbbing within them is a mini-world
where stoats
in stylish ermine
glissade a sinuous route through labyrinthine paths
and pirouetting whitrits dart and snap
at panicky voles.
Wrens and wagtails find small window-holes for nests,
green velvet mosses and the grey lace lichens
keep them dressed.

If you had told the dry-stane dykers
that they were sculptors
they would have laughed
and said that they were only builders
doing a job:
yet like the mystic standing stones
dykes have become an art form,
and when the sun shines on them
with the light of evening
their cold greyness
glows warm.
They come alive
and rise
like golden snakes
rippling their way upwards
to a high horizon.

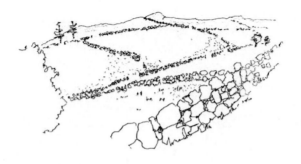

Force-field of the Breeze

The great white Phantoms are gathering on our moors.

From behind the Turnave and Glenward
and in the hidden Muirshiel valleys
and when you climb towards the summits of the Misty Law
and Windy Hill
you'll see them
three times as high as the slim cathedral spires
of the highest greenwood firs.

These Phantoms thrive
in a skeleton forest
Leviathans
with bleach-bone limbs exposed and dry
spectre heart-beats thumping in the sky above the grasslands
flailing arms bare of leaves
trying to reap in the force-field of the breeze.

Look!
The Phantoms are breeding,
seeding out into our wildest places
fast-growing
showing gaunt phantom faces
over the horizons of our hills
flaunting their whiteness
against mountain browns and greys –
a forest of bloodless aliens
sometimes uprooting
stealth-footing
nightmare haunting us
in the very high noon of our days.

No bowing to the phantom power,
no looking the other way.